This book belongs to

_____

Look Up and See

God's Glory Surrounds Me

Written and Illustrated by:

Jennifer Alford Walker

Dedications

This book is first, and foremost, dedicated to my Lord and Savior Jesus Christ, who through the empowering of His Holy Spirit gave me the words to write. I thank Him for allowing me to publish this and give Him Glory for it all. Ephesians 2:10

I would like to secondly dedicate this book to my own sweet children Emily, Joseph, and Grace. You have each taught me to always "Look Up!" You've reminded me the importance of noticing the small things, as well as the big things. Through every bug we discover, sunset we marvel, or bird on the feeder, I pray you will always "Look Up and See" how awesome our great God truly is!
-Mommy-
(Jennifer)

Look up and see the tall oak
How it grows so straight and tall.
As you look to the top,
It is so easy to feel very small.

Every year the trees lose all their leaves
They go from green to gold, then brown.
For life also has many seasons we know
And God's grace and love will constantly surround.

"And he shall be like a tree planted by the rivers of water,
that bring forth his fruit in his season;
his leaf also shall not wither;
and whatever he does shall prosper."
Psalm 1:3 (KJV)

The mountains whether they are giant snow-capped
Or soft, lush, rolling hills,
Are all grand and glorious in every way
That they bring such an amazing thrill.

The same God who created these
giant mountain tops
Is the same God who made me and you.
When we feel discouraged in our own very lives,
He only wants us to turn to him for renew.

"I look up to the mountains does my help come from there?
My help comes the Lord, who made heaven and earth."
Psalm 121:1-2 (NLT)

How many of us stand in awe
Of a beautiful sunrise or sunset?
And are immediately frozen
For a split second by its colorful bright vignette?

Red, orange, and yellow
Blue, pink, and purple
Shout with no words
God's glory is eternal.

"The heavens proclaim the glory of God;
the skies display his craftmanship."
Psalm 19:1 (NLT)

From the small primrose
To the massive sunflower,
We see with our own eyes
His amazing delicate power.

Every flower has a purpose
Within His own plan,
Which He formed on His own
Before the world even began.

*"There will be an abundance of flowers and singing
and joy...there the Lord will display his glory, the
splendor of our God."*
Isaiah 35:2 (NLT)

A river whether it is large or small
Flows gently or rushes fast.
It doesn't slow down or tarry around
Nor does it dwell on where it just passed.

We must never forget
all the ways God's provided,
Through sickness or difficult times.
When we remember how He helped through it all,
His glory will forever shine.

"When you go through deep waters I will be with you, when you go through rivers of difficulty you will not drown."
Isaiah 43:2 (NLT)

Birds come in all shapes, sizes, and colors
But there is one way that they are all the same.
God provides for them food and what they all need
None are hidden, and He knows them by name.

Just as He provides for a small little bird,
Won't He much more provide for you?
We need not worry about things big or small
His timing won't ever be overdue!

"Look at the birds. They don't plant or harvest or store food in barns, for your heavenly father feeds them. And aren't you far more valuable than they?"
Matthew 6:26 (NLT)

A gentle breeze blowing over a field
Seems to say stop and be still.
Feel the wind, smell the grass,
And look up to see the dance of the great daffodil.

God can speak to us in many ways
He asks us only to rest.
And as we listen, look, and feel
His promises will be manifest.

*"Be still and know that I am God. I will be exalted among
the nations, I will be exalted in all the earth."*
Psalm 46:10 (NIV)

As a storm rolls in, the sky gets very dark,
Lightning flashes and thunder rolls.
God is the creator of these mighty acts,
His power shows He's in control.

When the storms of life come our way,
His Holy Spirit is here to stay.
Even though we can't see Him
with our own eyes,
We know He's with us by our side.

"In times of trouble may the Lord answer your cry."
Psalm 20:1 (NLT)

God has placed us on this earth
For a limited number of days.
So, no matter what your season is,
Let His will be always in your gaze.

Time is such a funny thing,
It seems to either creep or hurry.
But no matter how long that you have,
Don't waste it, or then you'll be sorry.

"Make the most of every opportunity in these evil days."
Ephesians 5:16 (NIV)

"Teach us to number our days,
that we may gain a heart of wisdom."
Psalm 90:12 (NIV)

When you're constantly looking down at a screen
Can all His glory be fully seen?
God intends for our lives to be so much more,
Than to sit and soak looking down at the floor.

Time is so very precious;
It is a gift that is free.
So, let's use every moment
And not be absentee!

"Jesus said, "My purpose is to give them a rich and satisfying life." John 10:10 (NLT)

Bible Verses to Study

- Psalm 1:3: Look up and read this verse in your Bible and ask yourself how God wants you to be like a tree planted by rivers of water. Use your journal to record this verse and other things God speaks to you.

- Psalm 121: 1-2: Look up this verse and read in your Bible. How have you ever been discouraged? Use your journal to record this verse and then write a prayer to God thanking Him for helping you during that difficult time.

- Psalm 19:1: Look up this verse in your Bible and read. Think of a time you saw a beautiful sunrise or sunset. Write in your journal this verse and then watch out for the next beautiful one you see and write about it or paint a picture of it.

- Isaiah 35:2: Look up this verse and read in your Bible. Go outside and plant some flowers in a pot or flower bed. Plant some seeds and watch them grow over a few weeks and months. Use your journal to record the progress of their growth.

- Matthew 6:26: Look up and read this verse aloud. Write in your journal 5 things you may be worried about. Now pray and ask God to take the worry away and give you peace. Fill a birdfeeder with seeds and hang. Watch for birds to come and be reminded of God's providing of all your needs.

- Psalm 46:10: Read this verse and meditate on it by reading it 10 times. Spend time daily in quiet and pray. Use your journal to write prayers to God, or Bible verses in your journal.

- Ephesians 5:16: Read this verse and make a checklist of 5 things you need to complete. God wants us to be good stewards of everything He has given us, and time is one of those important things. Try to not waste time when you have a project to complete.

- John 10:10: Read this verse and discuss with a friend or parent what some "thieves" are in your life. What tries to steal the joy and peace that God gives to you?

To think about:

I believe it is important for everyone young and old to be an observer. Technology is a wonderful thing. We can communicate with friends from afar, or locate an address if we are lost, all from a single cell phone. How wonderful it can be, but oh how a cell phone can take us away from things that are truly important. On each page of this book there were things we all have seen before with our own eyes. Sometimes we see them but don't really see them for what they truly are; a display of God's glory.

The purpose of this book was to remind us all that God wants us to have a full life. He wants us to enjoy Him and all He's given us and praise Him for it all. It's easy to praise Him on the mountain and curse him during the storm. I pray that through every season of life we can all see that God has a purpose we must only seek Him to find that purpose.

I am guilty as everyone else by being sucked into technology, but this book has reminded me that to live the life God intends I must put Him first. I pray this book was an encouragement for you as it was for me. Use the previous page as a quiet time or devotion time for yourself or children.

----Jennifer (author, illustrator)

Birds
of the Air

Show Us God's
Love and Care

Written and
Illustrated by:
Jennifer
Alford Walker

Jennifer Walker is also the author and illustrator of *Birds of the Air*. She has always loved art and writing. Growing up in the country in Neshoba County, Mississippi, she spent a lot of time observing nature, and seeing God's glory in many aspects. She graduated from Mississippi University for Women with a degree in Art Education, then went on to Southwestern Baptist Theological Seminary to earn a master's degree in Christian Education, emphasizing in Childhood Education. She resides in Macon, GA where she, and her husband Glenn, are raising their three children, Emily, Joseph, and Grace. She homeschools and teaches art as well. She believes it is important to be an **observer** in life and notice the little things.

This book will help remind us to *Look Up and See*!